Rookie Read-About™ Science

It Could Still Be A Tree

By Allan Fowler

Images supplied by VALAN Photos

Consultants:
Robert L. Hillerich, Ph.D., Bowling Green
State University, Bowling Green, Ohio

Mary Nalbandian, Director of Science,
Chicago Public Schools, Chicago, Illinois

 CHILDRENS PRESS®
CHICAGO

Series cover and interior design by Sara Shelton

Library of Congress Cataloging-in-Publication Data

Fowler, Allan.
It could still be a tree / by Allan Fowler.
p.   cm.—(Rookie read-about science)
Summary: Identifies the characteristics of trees and provides
specific examples including the maple, evergreen, magnolia, and
redwood.
ISBN 0-516-04904-6
1. Trees—Juvenile literature. [1. Trees.] I. Title.
II. Series.
QK475.8.F68   1990   90-2207
582.16—dc20   CIP
                                                       AC

How do you know
it's a tree?

If it has a trunk of wood
covered with bark,

if green leaves grow
from its branches,

if it sends roots down
into the earth and it grows–
it's a tree.
It's a living tree!

But what if its leaves
aren't always green?
It could still be a tree

like this maple. When
fall comes, its leaves
turn red.

What if its branches are
sometimes bare?
It could still be a tree.
In winter, some trees lose
their leaves.

In spring, the leaves grow back again!

What if it stays
green all winter?
It could still be a tree

like an evergreen.

What if it's covered with
pretty flowers?
It could still be a tree

like a cherry tree.

A tree can grow in a place that's cold

or in a place that's warm.

A tree can grow in the
dry, dry desert
like a Joshua tree

or in water
like a cypress.
It's still a tree.

A tree can be as tall
as a redwood

or as tiny as a bonsai.

A tree can give us
a shady place to sit

or good things to eat
like apples or chestnuts

or acorns from oak trees.
Who eats acorns?
Squirrels eat them.

A tree can be home
for a family of birds.

So if you ever plant a tree,
you can say you built
a home.

Words You Know

leaves

branches

bark

trunk

roots

maple

evergreen

cherry tree

Joshua tree

cypress

redwood

bonsai

apple tree

31

Index

About the Author

Allan Fowler is a free-lance writer with a background in advertising. Born in New York, he lives in Chicago now and enjoys traveling.

Photo Credits

Valan—© Kennon Cooke, Cover, 15, 17, 23, 25, 26, 30 (bottom right), 31 (top left, bottom left, bottom right); © Thomas Kitchin, 4, 28; © Jean Bruneau, 5; © Pam E. Hickman, 6; © Stephen J. Krasemann, 9, 12, 20, 30 (bottom left), 31 (top right); © John Fowler, 11; © Harold V. Green, 18; © A. B. Joyce, 19; © Wouterloot-Gregoire, 21, 31 (center left), © Hälle Flygare, 22, 31 (center right); © J. A. Wilkinson, 24; © Pam Hickman, 27; © Lionel Bourque, 30 (top)

COVER: Red-leafed Maple